MW00417253

HEART
7 soft skill keys
CENTERED
to build effective teams
LEADERSHIP

Linda J. Merrill

Heart Centered Leadership
7 soft skills to build effective teams

Copyright © 2019 Linda Merrill

Editor: Qat Wanders and her team at Elite Authors

Cover Design by Dar Albert of WickedSmartDesigns.com
WickedSmartDesigns.com

Digital formatting by Nina Pierce of Seaside Publications
NinaPierce.com

ISBN: 978-1-7342222-1-0

Dedication

This book is dedicated to my family.

To my husband Mike, who has always been my rock. Thank you for encouraging me to be myself, for allowing me to grow in my own way, and for taking care of the boys while I traveled for work. You've helped me become the person I am today. I know it's not always easy to live with me, and I love you and appreciate all you do. Thank you for all you have done.

To my three sons, Alex, Jackson, and Nicholas, who are growing into their own. Thanks for being patient with me, and hopefully I have given you a way to find your own way to success and joy.

To my mom, who was an inspiration growing up. Thank you for showing that hard work pays off and that a single mom can work in a man's world and make a difference.

To God, for creating me and giving me a heart to see people as amazing creations in their messiness and gloriousness.

Contents

Introduction

Have you ever wanted to do something but didn't know what the future would look like? This happened to me when I decided to pursue a career in *something* with math and science. I was sixteen years old, trying to figure out what I wanted to be and what I wanted to do when going off to college. After a little bit of research into what careers could be a good fit (back then this was all done in the library—no internet!), I decided on engineering. I didn't know which type of engineering at the time, but I thought it was a good idea since I liked math and science and engineers made good money. I took Basic Programming during my senior year and was very successful at it. I decided that I would be an electrical engineer so I could learn more about computers, not just about software. If I didn't like working on hardware, I could always write software. But if I started in only software, I feared I would be stuck there forever.

I started working in optics and not in electrical engineering, but this came with the added benefit of learning electromagnetics. I was blessed to work with the CEO of the company I was at to learn how to design optical filters. It was a little unnerving to sit in his office all day, but I learned a lot. Unbeknownst to me, I was being groomed to be a program manager despite being brought on as a design engineer. I had no idea at the time, but I was talking to customers, doing bids, designing filters, putting together production plans, and making sure the final product was ready to go out. It was Project Management 101. At such a small company, we had to wear many hats. This turned out to be beneficial, as it started my career with a big-picture perspective—what it takes to go from bid to delivery.

I did this for about five years before changing fields into software engineering. I wrote firmware for a company then bounced around until I found something I liked. Once again, I found myself back at school, taking more programming classes. During this time, I met someone who worked for a big defense company. He said there were openings, so I decided to apply. I landed a job in the quality department and became a software quality engineer.

Here I learned so many valuable lessons. I learned how to evaluate other people's work without judgment. I learned what software processes meant. I learned how to write quality processes and how to bid on different-sized projects. I realized that it was really helpful to understand configuration management and also how to work across business teams. This stage of my career was all about communication—listening, asking lots of questions, and soaking in all the information I could. I had done this in the past, but this time was different. I was at a bigger company with more people, I was out of my comfort zone, and I had to show that I could learn quickly. I had to figure out how to help people across different teams, get them to produce the best product, and then deliver it to manufacturing.

After two years, my first son was born and I decided to work part-time. I chose to cut my hours so I could focus on being a mom, but I didn't want to give up my career because I had worked so hard for my engineering degree. I learned to become extremely efficient in the hours I had to complete tasks and quickly realized that if I could connect the right people with the right knowledge at the right time, project quality and timing would be better. As I learned to be efficient and streamline my processes to complete tasks, I began to see how this would work for whole teams.

In those early years, it was a struggle being a woman. I found I was not heard, respected, or appreciated at times—not so much by my boss, but by the teams I was serving. I had to come up with a strategy that would get me heard and taken seriously. I wanted to be respected and appreciated for the work I was doing and for what I was capable of. My self-confidence was already low, and these barriers didn't help. I had difficulties balancing being a mom and a career person, even though I worked only part-time. The demands were real on both sides. My job was my career, and although my hours were part-time, my attitude and work ethic were that of a full-time employee. I was trying to be superhuman, supermom, and wife.

The challenges became even more real when my husband told me he wanted out of our marriage. I was completely shattered. I crumbled, feeling like such a failure. Because I had built good relationships with the people I worked with, one of them rallied beside me to help me emotionally and spiritually. She introduced me to a healing priest. Each Sunday for four months, my two young sons and I went to worship services with her. I was now a single mom who had to keep it together for her boys. I am eternally grateful for my friend who encouraged me, walked with me, and guided me, helping me gain back my self-esteem. Every Sunday, the priest prayed with me and my boys.

At one of the services, I met a seminarian who said he would pray for the healing of my memories. He also challenged me to put my wedding band back on, go to confession, and fast and pray. Feeling desperate, I said I would do it. I wanted so badly for my marriage to work, and I missed my husband, my best friend. I also didn't want my sons to see me so broken down—I wanted them to rise from the ashes.

So I prayed with the seminarian for two hours, and together we walked through my entire life, from the very beginning in my mother's womb to present. He instructed me to take Jesus with me to the places of suffering in my soul. And so I did. When we were almost done praying, I felt my head spinning—like Linda Blair's in *The Exorcist*—and then I sensed a hand reach into my spinning head and pull out all my pain, suffering, hurt, and trauma. They were gone. I dropped to the floor and felt completely at peace. I felt loved and accepted for the first time in my life.

I found my confidence, my purpose—which was always there—but also a deeper faith. From that day on, I was a new creation. The possibilities were endless. My struggles remained, but I had the courage and strength to deal with them head-on because I knew I was loved and that Jesus had me. I walked a little taller and began to love people deeper. My husband and I began our journey of reconciliation. We had our third son and created our life together.

How does this pertain to leading teams and promoting efficiency and teamwork? Well, from here I had a deeper sense that all people deserve to be heard, loved, accepted, and appreciated.

I continued to work part-time while raising my kids. I coached them in soccer, baseball, and basketball, and helped them unlock their potential and work as a team. I stayed at that defense company for seventeen years but eventually decided to take a leap of faith and work in the automotive industry. I didn't know much about the automotive field, but the sensor programs I would be working on were similar radar systems I worked within defense, so I thought I'd be up to the challenge.

It was an international company, and I was told I would have to travel maybe three times per year to do audits in manufacturing plants to ensure the configuration management system was working. Within a month of starting at the company, we had an Automotive SPICE assessment. Although I didn't know what this was, I knew about assessments and audits. I spent my first two weeks learning the processes and creating matrices and maps to capture what the previous software quality engineer had done before me. The resulting document was so useful that I put it up in my office, and the development engineers asked for copies of their own.

Not only did this simple task help me learn about the team and the whole system in a short amount of time, but the other team members also gained a new perspective on their work. When the SPICE assessment happened, we passed no problem.

My boss and the team were impressed with how I handled the audit questions, so they asked me to go to the Michigan office and audit the processes there. This US site was working closely with a site in Germany, so I started digging into the processes and tried to figure out if they worked together or not. I learned that the two sites released software differently and hardly communicated with each other. I documented what I found and worked with the technical lead to figure out what could be done. He then asked me to join him at customer meetings being held in the German office.

This was my first international trip for work and my first experience with co-located teams. I had never been to Germany and had no idea what to expect. It seemed like an adventure and a way to step out of my comfort zone. I certainly had to put my faith in God to keep me safe and to help me get around (not much English on the signs and roadways). When I landed, I met up with the project team leader, and we headed to the manufacturing plant. I was exhausted, but my adrenaline was pumping. After a two-hour drive, we met with a customer and had some other meetings before I pulled myself away to catch up on some much-needed sleep.

The next day, we walked the manufacturing line where I witnessed the customer's experience with manufacturing firsthand. There were cobwebs on the automated machines. This was a concern. The machines were supposed to be cleaned on a schedule, but the schedule was seemingly ignored. However, the customer remained impressed by the flow of work.

I met the plant's quality manager and the industrial engineers responsible for the lines. I was impressed by their English but was surprised when they would apologize for it. I realized then that we all have insecurities and that if we are kind and understanding, it would be much easier to get along and work together. I didn't speak or understand any German, so their ability to speak English, even imperfectly, meant they were better off than me. While in Germany, I was, in a sense, an outsider. I began to appreciate what it must feel like for people who come to the US and don't speak or understand English. How hard it must be for them to get around.

With my first international experience, I ultimately learned humility. I had to find people who spoke English to order food and to find out what was on menus, but I quickly realized that body language is very effective for communication. Most of the time, I talk with my hands, especially when describing something. This helped when asking for a knife or directions, but I still couldn't figure everything out on my own and often had to ask for help. I also had to be aware of my surroundings constantly to ensure my safety when I was alone.

But I made it, and the trip was a success. I met with the most senior quality engineer and asked lots of questions about the process he and the team followed. We shared insights and began to build a working relationship that would prove to be fruitful in process efficiency. I realized at this point that the team was floundering without a leader. The quality engineers had different job descriptions and expectations than I was used to. And as we talked, I felt strongly that I needed to bring listening, acceptance, appreciation, and love to others. I could help them and guide them, and they could teach me about their way of doing business and their culture. To me, this was a win-win. I began to create a communication plan, job descriptions, and an organization structure to present to the leadership team.

In the following months, I reached out to the quality director, the group quality director, and whoever else would listen to present my thoughts on how to create an organization that worked together and gave the quality engineers a sense of purpose and space to do their jobs. I coordinated a global quality meeting and invited quality managers in other parts of our division to come to the workshop. This was the first time the global team of quality engineers and managers met, and the whole process was approved and accepted by leadership. The quality guys were so happy to be able to meet and discuss what was going on. They were starving for someone to lead them. One of the team members from Ireland asked if I would be their leader. They needed someone to guide, mentor, and encourage them.

I wanted to help, and this would allow me to live my purpose. I began to live out a set of principles that would prove effective in gathering information, leading engineers and leaders, mentoring junior engineers, and leading an organization that spanned the globe. My goal is to share the experience and insights I gained while leading this team to show you how to create a cohesive team united by a shared purpose. I will also provide practical activities you can use daily to help you and your teams be successful.

If you're working with international, diverse, or co-located teams, I hope this will inspire you, leaving you with an action plan you can use daily and monthly with your team.

Chapter 1

Defining L.E.A.D.E.R.S.

ANYONE WHO TAKES RESPONSIBILITY FOR
FINDING THE POTENTIAL IN PEOPLE AND
PROCESSES AND HAS THE COURAGE TO
DEVELOP THAT POTENTIAL.

What or who do you think of when you hear the word *leader*? Take a few seconds to jot down what your definition of a leader is. Then think of someone you know who doesn't meet that definition. Maybe this is someone you work with or have worked for. Next, think of someone who *does* fit that definition. Jot down who they are. Then write down the qualities they have that make them a great leader.

Over the years, I have worked with some great leaders and some not-so-great leaders. Great leaders have heart. They care for people and want the best for them. Great leaders guide others, mentor or coach them, and tell the truth even if it is a little painful, all in a spirit of care and building up others. A leader could be someone responsible for a team—a manager—or someone who is part of a team. Some managers are leaders and some managers are not. Personally, I like to work for managers who are also leaders.

But what's the difference between a leader and a manager? There are some similarities for sure, but let's break them down. A manager is a person who conducts business, controls resources and expenditures, or (in sports) is in charge of training an athlete or a team. A leader is the one in charge, the person who convinces other people to follow. A great leader inspires confidence in other people and moves them to action.

The difference here is subtle but important. A manager is someone with authority given by their position, but they may not be all that inspiring—that is, they may or may not be a good leader. I have certainly had some good managers, but let's just say there are others I would not want to work for again.

Why do some people become managers even though they aren't good leaders? Some managers gain their position of authority thanks to their education (e.g., having a master's in business management). Others do well in their job and get promoted, and others simply have aspirations to manage people and doggedly pursue manager positions. But once some of these individuals become managers, they may not have the skills to inspire those they manage.

Having managed others throughout my career, I've done a lot of thinking about the kind of manager I want to be. Do I want to be like my boss or do something different? Does my boss manage with respect and empathy, or does my boss have a command-and-control type of style that I do not want to emulate? I do not work well in a command-and-control environment. I like guidance, but I also like the chance to be autonomous and figure things out on my own. As I manage others, I am therefore conscious of the environment I am creating.

If you are aspiring to be a manager, be reflective in this same way and think about the characteristics of the great managers you have worked for. Gaining these qualities is something to aspire to if you don't have them already. If you do have them and have been successful in managing teams, then maybe this book isn't for you. But if you haven't been as successful as you want to be, or if you are working on moving up the career path, keep reading. I hope that you will find some nuggets of wisdom to help you on your journey.

But again, leaders are not necessarily managers, and managers are not necessarily leaders. You could be a leader even if you don't manage people. Do you lead your friends or family? Do you take charge of events and make them engaging? These are ways to lead.

This book is about digging a little deeper into what it means to be a leader. LEADERS is a convenient acronym to remember what it takes to lead. Let's break it down:

Listen

Educate

Appreciate

Diplomat

Empower

Rejuvenate

Support

Throughout this book, we will dive into each one of these letters as it pertains to working with cross-functional teams, international teams, co-located teams, and diverse teams—any team. I will share with you my experience and some tools to master each of the areas we cover.

Hopefully, you have been thinking about the great leaders you know and have written down what characteristics they possess, as I suggested above. This will allow you to come back to them as you continue to read through the book. I want you to discover that inside of you is a leader. Being a great leader is not necessarily the result of a natural-born—I am sure you have heard that leaders are made. Some people certainly have natural talents and grow up in environments that cultivate leadership, but by following the LEADERS philosophy, you just might find you have what it takes to be a great leader without any of that. I hope you are willing to take this journey with me as I share my experience in leading teams to their full potential.

I also hope you discover the many gifts and talents you already have so that you can begin to appreciate and mentor the people around you, no matter where you are in your leadership journey. Soon enough you'll be encouraging your teams, colleagues, or family to be the best versions of themselves while meeting or exceeding the goals set for yourself.

Chapter 2

LISTEN (from the heart)

TO GIVE ATTENTION WITH THE EAR; ATTEND
CLOSELY FOR THE PURPOSE OF HEARING;
GIVE EAR.

*My dear brothers and sisters, take note of this:
Everyone should be quick to listen, slow to
speak and slow to become angry.* ~James 1:19

I've been curious about other cultures, nationalities, and
people in general for as long as I can remember. I used
to ask my mom all the time, "Who's that? Where'd they
come from? Do you know their parents? Do you know
them? Why do they go there?" (It used to drive her
crazy.) But my curiosity didn't stop with people. From
an early age, I developed a curiosity about almost
everything. At the same time, I was taught that children
were to be seen but not heard. I figured that if I was not
supposed to be heard, it was best to sit near adults and
listen and feed that curiosity. Sometimes they wouldn't
even know I was there. I figured out at an early age that
when you listen, you learn all kinds of things.

One day, I discovered some new kids were moving into the neighborhood. They came from Cambodia and didn't speak English, which immediately made them stand out from everybody else around. It seemed that nobody wanted to talk to them. I, five years old and curious, went over, knocked on their door, and asked to meet the children. The parents were very excited because their kids had no friends. And that was the beginning of our friendship.

During this time, the neighbor kids taught me about their culture, and I helped them learn English. The parents didn't speak English very well, but that didn't matter. We still found ways to communicate with each other. I was so little that all I knew was I liked them and they were nice to me. I discovered that the more time I spent with my new friends, the more other kids would ask me about why I played with them. I would share how nice and fun they were, and then more kids started playing with us at the playground or in the fields. My new friends eventually joined us at church, too. There was a large youth program, and the pastor included all of us, even those who did not yet officially belong to the church. After I invited the new neighbors to more and more activities, they were accepted not only in our neighborhood and church but at school, too.

By taking an interest in my new neighbors and seeking to understand their culture, I practiced the *L* of

LEADERS—Listen. I began to listen from my heart. I heard the words, but I also heard something more. I watched their body language and I tried to understand their meaning, not just the words. I took what a learned in church to heart: "Call to me and I will answer you and tell you great and unsearchable things you do not know" (Jeremiah 33:3). This listening was not always easy, but I felt a strong desire to understand them and their culture. I wanted to know what they are saying. I wanted to be able to play and make new friends.

I also spent a lot of time alone as a child—quiet time. My favorite place was at church and being with Jesus. I wanted to always be with him. In the quiet stillness, I felt I could hear him, or at least feel him. In these quiet moments, I was also learning to listen from my heart. In Sunday school, I was taught that Jesus could be the best friend ever. I greatly wanted to have friends. Knowing that Jesus was different, I also felt different, so maybe people from other places also felt different. How could I understand them if we didn't speak the same language? Heart language, as I called it then, was the way.

I began to ask God to help me to understand and be open to other people. I remember that my parents had gone to see Up with People and bought the album. If you have never heard them or seen them, they are a group of young adults between the ages of eighteen and twenty-five of different nationalities, and they perform all around the world, One of the songs, "What Color Is God's skin?" touched my heart with its lyrics: "It's black, brown. It is yellow. It is red. It is white. Everyone is the same in the good Lord's sight." I thought if God sees us all the same, then who am I to judge. People are people. Quite the lesson for a little girl. I appreciate my parents for playing this album many times throughout my childhood years. Later in college, I got to see Up with People myself, and they still sang this song.

When I was in college, most of my professors were different nationalities. Trying to understand those who spoke English as a second language during my freshman year of college was a little difficult. Engineering school wasn't easy to begin with and this created an additional barrier. During class on Fortran, a computer language I knew nothing about, I hardly ever understood what the professor was saying. It took me almost the whole semester to figure out one sentence that he always asked in class: "Am I correct?" But the added challenge of this language barrier made me listen. I had to pay attention in class if I wanted to do well.

Once I figured out what my professor was saying, I felt I could share with other students my difficulty. Then I learned they too had the same issue. I began to open my ears and eyes more to the people around me to see and hear what they were struggling with so I could help them understand. I internalized the notion that everyone wants to be understood and heard, and sometimes there are barriers that stop this from happening. I searched inside myself to find a solution to the communication problem my classmates and I were facing. I started to ask people whether they wanted to study together to gain clarity on assignments, and I reached out to teachers more often for clarification so I could report back to my friends.

I also started paying attention to body language. This helped when a teacher would explain a concept. I would look around the room to see the body language and facial expressions of my classmates. If it seemed like no one understood, I would ask the professor a question for clarification. This opened up more questions from others, and we all benefited. Many students spoke English as a second language as well, and these questions helped them as well. It's affirming to hear others ask questions when you are confused.

Every person deserves to be accepted and loved. Whether you're young or old, or from one place or another, every person deserves to be valued for who they are. What makes us special is that we are all unique in our own way. We all have gifts and talents that we bring to the table. Because of this, we can embrace each other's differences and embrace our human dignity.

I found this to be true once I started working. As a female engineer, I was bullied by people who thought I slept with one of the bosses to get my position or receive my one-on-one training with the CEO. None of that, of course, was true, but I still was the topic of a lot of gossip. There weren't that many female engineers at the time, and it was clear that the gossipers just didn't understand how to value differences or people as they are. It is important to accept that we can learn and grow from each other, embrace each other's differences, and help each other to be the best versions of ourselves. When we can be open to each other and listen and appreciate each other's worlds, lives can be changed.

Luckily for me, that CEO did take the time to teach me valuable skills: how to design thin film coatings, how to bid new jobs, and how to communicate with our customers. He was always generous with his time, no matter the questions I had, and it seemed he wanted me to be successful. I am grateful for all he taught me as a new engineer and for covertly making me a project manager right out of college. I had no clue what I was doing, but I quickly learned because that CEO took the time to mentor me. I truly see him as a saint because he took care of his people. At the time, we didn't pay anything for health care—he covered all of it. He would make sure no one got laid off during the difficult times, and he even paid an employee's salary for two years while she went through chemotherapy. He valued all his people, even if some of his employees and managers did not.

The truth is, even with the difficulties I faced, so many good things came from these experiences. I was blessed to meet my husband, learn from some really smart people who took a chance on me, and then was able to move on to another company with confidence in my abilities, my curious nature, and my listening heart. Although this first job was challenging, I learned to embrace the differences of everybody who was there. Using the listening skills I had developed, I began to value everyone and what they brought to the work we did. At times, they would drive me crazy with their idiosyncrasies, the way they communicated, or their cliques, but in the end, it all worked out.

Talking to customers regularly and having to listen to their needs and concerns about design products that would work in their system taught me to listen not only to their words but also at a deeper level. Sometimes the customer specifications weren't enough, so asking the right questions to get more information was necessary to see if our design would help them. When I was working on a quote, I would have to listen and understand clearly their financial constraints and delivery dates. All of this was beneficial early on. By the time a quote was ready to go to the customer, there was a good sense within the company of what it was going to cost and how long it was going to take. Everybody was on board. What a true gift.

I was able to create good relationships with customers, which produced repeat business and on-time deliveries with quality products. By truly listening to what they wanted, I helped them to meet their schedules and needs. I began to help others with their bids and helped the quality team understand customer needs so they could inspect the product and be prepared for the workload coming to them for delivery. I was leading the team even though I wasn't a manager.

A good leader listens to the whole team and allows them to be part of the process. Using your listening skills, you will have a better understanding of what the whole team needs. A good leader realizes that everyone brings something to the table. By giving people the space to share, you are providing an atmosphere of teamwork. Listening to their ideas and solutions to problems, everyone will feel part of the project and more willing to meet customer and delivery needs. With everyone working together, you can get your product out the door with minimal arguing, struggle, or delays. There will still be challenges, of course, but when the leader provides space for open communication and listens, the ability to mitigate issues can happen much quicker.

The takeaway here is that communication is important but listening to what is said is key.

Gathering data is another way to listen. Sometimes the data speaks loudest—people usually hear what the data says. This is true for throughput yields and the timing of how long each manufacturing process takes. This is also true for the final step of quality control and going back to the specifications, measuring common requirements, delivery times, and how long quality control spends on projects. Data can also tell us how we are doing as leaders. If we are capturing the correct information, we can figure out what it is saying. This is another way of listening.

By encouraging communication and listening to different departments who didn't necessarily talk to each other, I was becoming a bridge within the company. I learned that being kind and asking questions about what people did and how they worked helped employees appreciate their jobs. As they explained their work to me, they became excited and they wanted to help. They wanted to make sure the customer was happy. Asking for their help opened up their world as well as mine. Life is not a one-man show (or a one-woman show). It takes the whole system—the human system—to get the job done. Sometimes the ideas that came from one department would help another. Unfortunately, there was a lot of running around every day. I hadn't yet learned the power of a whole-system meeting, a kickoff meeting, or other processes that would have been so much more beneficial to these teams. However, being the bridge and really listening to each team's needs created more of a team environment and a more fun place to work because we knew each other. Again, the key here is to listen and to encourage listening.

Sometimes when we are listening, we jump to conclusions and interrupt others. I do that more often than I would like to admit. To be a better listener, I always practice keeping my mouth shut and focusing on the person speaking. I also journal to practice listening. This journaling usually involves Lectio Divina—taking a scripture and reading it three times in a row, at which point a word or phrase will jump out at me. I write that in my journal, stay silent, and go deep within to listen to my heart and the Holy Spirit about what the scripture means for the day. Then I write my thoughts in my journal. I have found this practice has given me a better understanding of things that I wouldn't have otherwise known. For example, I've gained insights about my team, their needs, and those of projects. By doing this, I've discovered there is a scripture passage for every single situation, be it about work, relationships, family, or money.

Listening—and it is an action (verb)—takes practice, but if you are willing to do so, you will gain new experiences. You will begin to have a new understanding of the people you are working with. You just might find yourself surprised about what you learn, and your world will change. You may even find you have more patience and peace with even the most difficult team and family members. By listening, you can then lead in a more compassionate and heartfelt way that your team and family will appreciate.

> *Lord, hear my prayer, listen to my cry for mercy; in your faithfulness and righteousness come to my relief.* ~Psalm 143:1

Practice Exercise 1:
The Art of Listening

Make sure you have a quiet space to sit and relax and have pen before you start the following exercises.

- Now close your eyes and take a deep breath. As you breathe, notice what you hear. Then notice what sounds you hear around you.
- Be aware of the softest, smallest voice you hear.
- Try to ignore the loud ones and really dig deep to hear the small voice inside you.

    - When you hear it, on the following page, take a moment to write down what you hear.

Practice Exercise 2:
Listening to Our Team

- Now close your eyes and take a deep breath. As you breathe, think about one of your team members or someone you influence.

- Focus on this person and recall previous conversations, noticing what was being said or not said. Write down what you recall this person needing from you, your organization, or someone in your family. How can you help?

- Try to remember the scene of the conversation—the sounds, the body language, the tone of the conversation.

- Is there something you could do for this person?

- Be aware of the softest, smallest voice. Try to ignore the loud ones and really dig deep to hear the small voice inside you.

- When you hear it, write it down.

You can repeat this exercise for everyone on your team or in your family.

Practice this for thirty-days and see where this life leads you and your relationships with your team, co-workers, family and friends.

I would love to hear from you as you begin this journey of heart listening. Your feedback is always welcome, especially if it will improve this process for yourself and others.

Please feel free to email me
linda.j.merrill@pontemvitae.com

Chapter 3

EDUCATE

TO PROVIDE WITH KNOWLEDGE OR
TRAINING IN A PARTICULAR AREA OR FOR A
PARTICULAR PURPOSE.

*Apply your heart to instruction and your ear to
words of knowledge.* ~Proverbs 23:12

*Give instruction to a wise man, and he will be
still wiser; teach a righteous man, and he will
increase in learning.* ~Proverbs 9:9

*Let the wise hear and increase in learning, and
the one who understands obtain guidance.*
~Proverbs 1:5

Going to school or taking skill-based classes are ways
people educate themselves about their careers or a
particular area of expertise. But how do we educate
ourselves about a new subject outside the classroom?
How do we figure out how to work with people who
don't speak English? Today, the internet, thanks to

platforms like YouTube and Google, makes it easier than ever to learn. Still, we sometimes need to speak with people face-to-face to truly learn. Sometimes we need to practice the art of listening to ask questions that can help us learn. I found that asking my team members lots of questions was the best way to find out their needs and learn about the different work cultures of each team. Doing this as a leader can give you a sense of the big picture within your company, which can also make you a bridge between different work disciplines.

Asking questions to gain this knowledge takes some humility and guts. When I first visited Germany, I asked people who had gone before me about German culture. What was common for the people of Germany? What was their work ethic? How did they communicate? I also read a book on culture ethics specific to Germany so that I could understand what was acceptable. While educating myself, I had to take some criticism when I handled situations differently than was expected. For instance, I learned that saying "I think" when you have an answer to a solution does not translate well from English to German because it sounds as if you only have an idea, not a solution. I had to change my phrasing to share my solutions to problems. Getting to that point took a lot of humility, practice, and questions of my team members from Germany. This kind of education is vital to business.

When you travel, experience other cultures, and have an open mind, you will be more in tune with your team and their needs. By having this kind of worldly education, you will appear as more of an authority figure when sharing ideas with your team. This work to understand people is just as important as spending time studying in your discipline to become the expert and leader in your industry and background.

However, this kind of education is more heart-centered as you learn and discover people and cultures. If you take a real interest in others and learn about them by asking questions, you will find a new world opened up for them and you. By doing this for myself, I was able to bridge gaps in processes across disciplines and connect people who needed to work together. I educated myself on company policies and was able to teach them to different teams, leading them to a better understanding in their own style and to work together, no matter where they were.

Asking lots of questions and then listening to the answers is one way to educate yourself. Just asking questions for the sake of asking questions doesn't serve anyone. The point here is to educate yourself. For example, you might need to understand company standard processes, the people who follow the processes, customer needs, team needs, company expectations, etc.

However, there are usually reading materials you can also use to get a sense of these company expectations. You can also read about different cultures and countries if you work with diverse teams. The bottom line: arm yourself with knowledge. Educating yourself on the project scope, financials, and customer specifications keep you on top of what is needed for the job and how you can help your team perform at its best.

Furthermore, share information with the team so everyone on the project is educated. If possible, share the knowledge at the beginning of a project and when new people come on board. By being an example of learning, you will open the door for your team to do the same. It is also helpful to have education materials readily available for the team in a central location. Having a list of where all documentation can be found or training materials for the team is also useful to everyone. Supplying books or online resources approved by the company is also beneficial. Additionally, I believe it is also important to allow your team time for education. Some companies will pay for outside training or have internal training programs. Listen to your team about what they need, and if possible, provide the training they need or send them to where they can get it.

Education does not always mean going to school. Sometimes life can be the best teacher. Learning from past mistakes or even successes can help the future of your team. Life and work are journeys of their own.

Following is an example of a time when I educated myself:

I was chatting online with a former coworker from overseas, and she said she was having feast days. Not being Muslim, I asked her what feast day she was celebrating. Hajj, she replied. I immediately got on Google and searched "Hajj and the feast days" to see what the feast days meant. When we spoke on the phone the next day, I could ask her more questions. I found out that Muslims must travel at least once during their lifetime travel to Mecca. I knew from years ago but didn't realize there was a feast associated with it. I asked her if she had made her pilgrimage yet and found that she had not but had plans to.

I would not have known anything of this had I not educated myself. I am not saying you have to believe in what others believe, but educating yourself opens up conversation and allows for connection and acceptance of other people. Both of us enjoy each other's perspective and prayer lives even though we have different beliefs. We can still have amazing dialog and openness and appreciate where each other is coming from. This connection and appreciation for her have created a safe space for open dialog and for sharing ideas and beliefs, creating trust. Throughout our time working together, I've learned and recognized her strengths, enabling me to better encourage and include her and the whole team in our work. Ultimately, she came up with some great process ideas and felt empowered to work with me and the team to meet our goal of setting up quality processes across our division. By creating a space of open dialog and leading each team member to do the same as a group, we were not only performing at a high level—we were becoming more of a family with a mission to better ourselves, each other, and the company. Because I believe in leading by example, the whole team was open and created safe spaces at different sites, and the communication across the projects and disciplines began to improve. When you can take a step back and educate yourself about the differences between people and embrace those differences, you can lead your team to improve performance. In all honesty, they will make *you* look good as the manager.

It does make a difference when you value the whole person. When you are leading a team and embrace each person fully, you will see their strengths and be able to encourage them to use those strengths for their good and the good of the company. You can build on their strengths and provide feedback on what is working and be open about areas that need improvement. Don't just know about your team members' jobs, how they react, or what they do for you. Find out who they are. Deep down in their soul, who are they? This is where being curious is a benefit. When you value the whole person and you understand who people are, it helps them become better versions of themselves in the safe place you've created. They become willing to answer questions to get them to think and reflect on the direction of their careers or lives. You can lead them to discover what's within themselves and bring the best out of them. relationship as well.

Practice Exercise 3:
Education

Think about your team and something you'd like to teach them or something you want to learn.

- What avenues of learning can you take to educate yourself about how to improve your company's processes or your work within your team?

- Write down how you will get the skills or knowledge you need.

- How can you also bring this knowledge or these new skills to your team?

- Do you need to create a training?

- Jot down your ideas here and plan when you will do this.

Chapter 4

APPRECIATE

TO BE GRATEFUL OR THANKFUL FOR.

Finally, brothers, whatever is true, whatever is honorable, whatever is just, whatever is pure, whatever is lovely, whatever is commendable, if there is any excellence, if there is anything worthy of praise, think about these things.
                                        ~Philippians 4:8

For what thanksgiving can we return to God for you, for all the joy that we feel for your sake before our God.   ~1 Thessalonians 3:9

Valuing the uniqueness of everybody's role makes your job even easier, and the next step is to appreciate those people for who they are. Appreciating the work people do and what people bring to the table from their experiences and educational background means, in part, spending time figuring out what makes them tick. Sometimes it also means finding out about their families or the hobbies they have. Spending a little extra time after work or during lunch to find out more about your team members lets them know you care about them. These interactions build trust and a willingness to share and be open. When there are difficulties on the job or there is a need to be met, employees who feel heard and trusted are more open to sharing their ideas and to help solve problems. Remember, we are building up the human system in the workplace along with the "machine" systems.

So how do you position yourself to ask lots of questions, be curious, and ensure that you're appreciating your team and coworkers? A best practice is to spend some time meditating and reflecting. This allows you to see yourself more clearly but also clears your mind to be fully present in the moment. This will spill into your workday and help you be present with your coworkers. Being present is when you are totally focused on the person—no distractions from phones or computers, and using the skill of listening to focus on the other person. This happens more naturally when we're true to ourselves and are genuinely inquisitive about other people, making it much easier to appreciate them for who they are. I'm not perfect, and I don't think anyone is, so I always ask myself: "Who am I to judge?" My role is to appreciate and accept not only myself but others.

There are different methodologies in software development. Using the AGILE software development methodology, we can learn how to appreciate our teams.

This methodology involves asking questions, such as: What does the team do well together? Asking each team member to answer this brings appreciation and value to the team. When team members can recognize each other and appreciate the work they have done together, they are more apt to appreciate each other's inputs.

When there are team members from different parts of the world or even just different parts of development teams, it's really important to understand each person's role and background. A way to do that, as I've said, is to ask lots of questions and be curious. Some questions I like to ask are: What's important to you in this project? How do you like to add value? How do you like to be seen? As a contributor? As a leader? How do you see yourself?"

Then I let them answer. I also ask lots of questions about what they like to do and how they interact with their friends, just find out who they are. Do they have a big family? A small family? Do they like to hang out with their family? Who's the most important person in their family? If they don't have a family of their own, do they want one someday?

The key here is, again, not to judge. You don't want to judge their answers. We're really digging into who they are and what makes them tick. When you do ask these kinds of questions, really listen to their answers, and value who they are, you are lifting them up and allowing them to feel important to you. By actively listening, you allow them to just be and express who they are. By doing this, you are creating a safe space for them to be open to the work environment. Now, I'm not saying to probe deeply—some people are very private. But if they are willing to go deeper, feel free to walk that journey with them. But if not, still value that they don't want to share and do not judge. If they say they don't want to talk about it, say, "That's okay. I was just curious. No worries." Then you're accepting them.

Put the onus on you and not on them. This really helps in honoring the person's wishes. Honoring the people on the team means allowing them to open up if they so choose, but also not forcing them to. Either way, it's all OK. When they see that you care about them and that you value them, all is well. Just keep avoiding passing judgment, especially in the workplace, because everybody's there to do their job and work together (hopefully). When people come from different backgrounds, honoring everyone as human beings make it much easier for the team to be cohesive.

When accepting everyone for the gifts and talents they have, what can you do to appreciate the work they do? I've found recognizing people's talents at group meetings and workshops, or even phone calls and emails is a great way to show you're grateful for the work they've done. Even when someone may not be performing to their highest potential, I always find a way to appreciate something they do. A simple thank you for the work performed or acknowledging the time put into the work can go a long way.

If an employee reveals a strength when getting a task done, I make sure to mention that I am glad to have them on my team. I also make sure to note team members' strengths so I can provide them tasks that set them up for success, even if I have them push a bit beyond their current capability. I find that by encouraging people to step up, they eventually grow into the role or develop the technical understanding required. Of course, I don't leave them without a net—at least usually.

I had one employee who was in my product line but had a local boss from Cairo, a young engineer, who was very good and wanted to grow in his role. We brought him from Cairo to Germany to customer meetings to discuss the quality process he had been using on the project. We realized he was really great in front of the customer, and we had a need in the German office for someone just like him. He was willing to relocate, but since I lived in the US, and I was not always available to him during his first months in Germany. I knew he was capable, but he never had a leader who trusted or allowed him to think on his own. He was nervous but he did amazingly. He mentioned that he wished I had assigned him someone to mentor him, which is a great idea. However, he said if I had not given him the opportunity to grow (I knew he could do it, so I kept encouraging him and was available when he needed it most), he would not be stretched to learn new things and make decisions the program needed to be made. Now, he's an impressive engineer who has greatly helped the program and organization.

Of course, it is sometimes difficult not to judge, especially when you're an expert in the field. I sometimes feel this way when I get frustrated when my people don't follow the process they need to. I've had to hold team meetings, so as to not single anyone out, and then hold one-on-one meetings to coach on the correct processes to follow. This was challenging for some of the team members, as those who had been with the company for a long time hadn't been trained to work any other way. At times, I had to take a step back and educate myself on the process they had been using and then take the time to mentor and coach. Understanding that they did good work but just didn't know to do a certain process any different, helped me stay calm and avoid being too judgmental. By focusing on what I appreciated about their work, I had the opportunity during review time to show them where they shined and where they could improve. Balancing appreciation for their years of exceptional work with constructive criticism made our team strong, a voice for good, and a resource for other development teams.

Even if someone's work isn't to our own standards, we can take a step back and still appreciate all the work that has been done. There's always something positive to say. I will admit, there are times when this has been tough, but I always believed that my guys knew what they were doing and just needed a little guidance. In my heart, I wanted them to be their best selves and to think on their own. I was always available if they needed me for guidance. When they would ask questions, I would ask back, "What is your thought on how it should be handled? What would you do if I wasn't here or no one was around?" Then I would give them time to explain the situation and how they think it should be handled. Most of the time, just being a sounding board was very effective because they could think it through. Even if they were not right on target, I gained an opportunity to coach them through it.

This was the best part of my job. Seeing the team figure things out and have those aha moments made my day. By doing this, they were more willing to share their ideas and to raise concerns, giving them more of a voice in the programs they were assigned to. Their confidence grew, and they present information more clearly to the project managers and engineering teams.

By appreciating their thoughts and asking questions, I led in a way where everyone benefited. I also put in a good word with HR to make sure the team was taken care of financially and recognized for their exceptional work. I also took them out to dinner, if possible, as a thank you and to get feedback from them away from the office. I enjoy doing nice things for people, and when I got the opportunity to say thank you, I would do so. I believe that I opened my heart to them and was grateful not only for the opportunity to lead them but also for the work they did to make me look good. I still have a love for them all. They all became a big part of my life, and I wanted what was best for them. I carried an enthusiasm for the work we did and led them to catch this enthusiasm, so much so that it broke my heart to have to leave them (although I knew deep down they were a tight unit and could do the work without me).

I am grateful for that opportunity to lead such extraordinary people who were willing to go above and beyond, to accept my coaching, and to stretch themselves. I am proud of them all, and I wish them the best.

Practice Exercise 4:
The Art of Appreciation

*Is there someone on your team or in your family
that needs to be recognized or appreciated for a job
well done or for going above and beyond?*

- Write down the name of the person.

- Now write down the strengths that person used or any of the good qualities that person has.

- Write out that person's successes.

- Is there something you can give that person, such as public recognition?

- Write your ideas down here and pick one to implement this week.

Linda J. Merrill

Chapter 5

—◆—

DIPLOMAT

A PERSON WHO HELPS PEOPLE WITH
DIFFERENT POINTS OF VIEW FIND COMMON
GROUND.

> *I appeal to you, brothers, to watch out for those who cause divisions and create obstacles contrary to the doctrine that you have been taught; avoid them.* ~Romans 16:17

Ah, a diplomat—definitely something a leader needs to be, especially if the teams are large, cross-functional, or across oceans. Think of the best diplomats you know. The one that stands out the most to me is Mother Mary. She always welcomes everyone, no matter who they are. According to the Church, she has appeared to different cultures over the years. For instance, she showed up in Egypt, not only when she and Joseph fled to Egypt with Jesus but also later, as Our Lady of Zeitoun. She has also appeared in Fatima, Japan, France, and elsewhere, taking on the appearance of the people she's revealed to.

There are also stories throughout church history of Marian apparitions that appear to people in need. In 1531, it is said that Our Lady of Guadalupe appeared in a vision to a Mexican peasant, Juan Diego. She spoke to him in his native tongue and asked that a church be built at the site where she appeared. Church authorities wouldn't listen, and Juan Diego was sent away. Then Mary appeared to him again, telling him to gather flowers from the top of a hill that was usually barren. He followed her instructions and found roses that were not native to Mexico. She arranged the flowers in his *tilma* (cloak), and when Juan Diego opened the cloak in front of the archbishop, the flowers fell to the ground, and on the fabric was the image of the Virgin of Guadalupe (USA Today, February 12, 2016). She also appeared, according to church tradition, in Fatima, Portugal in 1917, predicting wars and a miracle of the sun.

There are many more stories of her apparitions, which you can research if you would like to know more. She is a diplomat who brings people together and joins them to a common goal. When working with international teams, I never traveled without her. I always asked her to help me understand the customs and culture and to hear what people were saying. I would pray on every flight for her protection and her guidance. I believe she gave me a diplomat's heart—the ability to understand all people and to appreciate them deeply.

I also think of Mahatma Gandhi as a diplomat, although he didn't officially have that title. He lived in Africa for a time and was persecuted and treated harshly and from this experience he decided to become a politician to end racism. He eventually returned to India Gandhi India in 1915. He brought an international reputation as a leading Indian nationalist, theorist and community organizer. (Wikipedia) During his life and even after death he continues to influence so many people. There are so many influential people who work with diverse groups, and it's easy to see they deserve the title of diplomat. With *diversity* as a major buzzword in business these days, these kinds of diplomats are more important than ever. But what does diversity really mean? Merriam-Webster defines *diversity* as "the condition of having or being composed of differing elements ... *especially*: the inclusion of different types of people (such as people of different races or cultures) in a group or organization." Yes, we have women and men on our teams. We have people from different countries, and we have people from different locations inside of our countries. Today's teams are truly diverse, with people of different sexes, genders, and nationalities all working together.

When you have a diverse team, you can look at it as a problem or a solution. I believe it is a solution because ideas come from many angles and different ways of thinking. For example, each country has a different way of looking at hierarchy. Depending on where you are, you may encounter different rules for organizations, rules for hiring, and role definitions. What's important is to educate yourself on these rules if you are working with people/teams from a country different than your own. Find out how people in that country define and assign roles, and what a team member can do when they have a certain role. Some countries—Germany, for example—are strict about the work a person can do based on the role he or she is assigned. It is important to know this because individuals may not be able to perform a specific function if it is not in their job description. Other places like the US don't do this unless you are part of a union. Being a diplomat means you are able to understand, communicate, and work within these sorts of constraints because you have researched (educated yourself) about where your team is located.

The next step is to take this knowledge and begin to engage the team. Recognize how they are working, or decide how you would like them to work. Do the teams work completely autonomously, or do they work interdependently? This is really key when you're leading these teams, because how they interact—who's doing what, who's responsible for what, or who ultimately owns the end product—is important to ensure each deliverable passes smoothly on to the next team in the line. It's really important to know how everyone is positioned in this regard.

For example, employees in Cairo work within a hierarchical society. There are positions of authority, and the people in those positions are respected automatically. People work hard to advance quickly so they can gain that respect. Appreciating this value system means recognizing the importance of being promoted within a year—two years tops— so, you need to look at what people are doing, how they're doing it, and how quickly you can promote them or recommend for promotion. If they're really good, you want to keep them. But if they do not feel they are advancing quickly enough, they may move on to a place where they get the promotion.

Understanding these sorts of expectations within various organizational structures is vital. If you're on a project, it's important to know who people report to and the appropriate ways to interact with them. This is true even here in the United States. Say there are two locations working together—one could be on the West Coast, and the other could be in the middle of the country. There will be differences in working behaviors and in who does what at these locations. Again, it's really important to know where people are coming from, what's important to them, and how they work in order to best distribute work and best utilize a team's diversity for the good for the project, the program, the product, and the customer.

This brings us to our next point. At the end of the day, there's a delivery to a customer, and that's where you need to be a diplomat as well. It's important to know as much about the customer as you can. Where are they located? Where are they going to be using this product? How do their teams interact? Do they have people who fill similar roles as the people on your team? Is there somebody that you need to talk to that maybe isn't sitting in the main office?

Questions, questions ... asking them is the only way to lead and to gain a grasp of the team and the work. Keep curiosity as a way of life in order to understand the project you're working on, the customer's needs, and what's important within different work cultures. Over the years, I have found that a yes in Chinese culture doesn't always mean people will do what you asked. It means they understood and heard you. It is important to be a diplomat and use the right language when asking questions and looking for clarity. Did they understand your request? As a leader, it's really important for you to know these things, so do research on the cultures of places where you work, and of course, ask lots of questions. Staying curious is so important because if you really genuinely want to know a person or culture, you can get your answers even without reading books (but you should read them anyway!). Educate, educate, educate. Being a diplomat means you understand how business is conducted anywhere you work and can bridge the gap between cultures.

When you educate yourself, arm yourself with the understanding that a curious mind and a genuine love for people will increase your confidence and the respect others have for you. Being a diplomat means you can listen to all people, see where they are coming from, and fill in gaps or bring clarity when needed. The first three keys (listen, educate, and appreciate) are necessary to becoming a diplomat. When you follow the first three keys and can communicate with your heart, you become the bridge between people and processes. This has helped me in my career over the years. Genuinely honoring others—even if I messed up, didn't quite follow their customs, or did things differently than they expected— they helped make things work out. By showing love in your work, you open a door to discussion and acceptance. I have found that most people want the same things in life. After all, we are all human even though we live in different locations.

It's also really important to have clear role distinctions. Let me explain this. For example, if you have software quality engineers in two locations, and they're on the same project, it's really important to distinguish who is responsible for what upfront. Now, this works really well if the team can get together at the beginning of a project. It's always good to have a face-to-face kickoff meeting. People will ultimately work so much better together when there are face-to-face encounters. However, that's not always easy or practical. The next best thing would be to hold a virtual meeting where everyone can see each other (think Skype, Web-X, or Zoom).

If there are processes already in place for duplicated roles, then ensure they are consistent across the sites. If they are, then the next step is to see where there are overlaps. It's best to have a dialogue with people in overlapping roles to find out how each of them performs their job duties and what they see as their responsibilities. Allow each of them to share so they can contribute and decide who will be accountable for each part of the process. This way, they have ownership of the work and will in turn work better together, no matter where they're located. Having them contribute and be heard is much more effective than telling them what to do. (This is *empower*ment, the next key.) The important points are to have as little overlap as possible and to have everyone engaged. Some overlap may be inevitable, but I have found that doing this at the beginning of a project means each person has a better chance of understanding the scope of their work and holding themselves and others accountable. People working together in this way helps ensure that the product is developed, delivered to the customer, or passed on to the next step with minimal issues.

Working in this way is especially helpful for co-located teams and teams with utilizing multiple disciplines in each location. If roles are well defined and cooperation and communication across the teams are facilitated at the beginning, a project is more likely to be successful. Isn't that what we are all working toward, successful projects and successful teams? Establishing kickoff meetings and open and honest communication from the beginning, with clear role definitions and accountability to activities, is the job of an empowering diplomat. All of these efforts help boost people's confidence because they know what they are supposed to produce and accomplish over the life of the project.

Understanding where your team is, providing clear role definitions, and learning how each culture operates will benefit the whole system. One thing that I learned in my travels is that the French and Germans sometimes have difficulty working together. This animosity dates back to the Franco-Prussian War. Of course, there weren't always difficulties, and when there was, it had nothing to do with work or with the individuals. Any strife was simply a consequence of history. I didn't know this before I traveled, but as I observed people and heard conversations, I realized the historical roots of this tension at work. Overall, everyone wanted to do their work, provide quality products, and be happy. If your teams are co-located, it's important to understand where they're coming from, right? By bringing teams face-to-face, they see each other as human beings, not as citizens of a particular country. Most of us will honor the human, and it doesn't matter where you're from. As a leader, it's important to get the team together, even if not physically or face-to-face. Sometimes a video conference or a conference call is all you need. It's all about asking the question: How can each of these diverse cultures work together, and how can we bring about open and honest communication for the life of the project?

Practice Exercise 5:
Diplomat

Schedule a face-to-face meeting with your team.

- If this is not possible, schedule a Zoom or Skype call, so that you can see each other.

- On the following page, create your agenda. Use this opportunity to get your team on the same page, and create an hour-long team-building exercise to identify strengths and set goals.

(*Note*: I offer team building workshops to help you create working relationships that are more open and honest. Visit www.PontemVitae.com for booking or email at info@pontemvitae.com if you'd like more information.)

Chapter 6

---◆————————————◆---

EMPOWER

TO HELP PEOPLE MEET THEIR POTENTIAL
AND GROW AS INDIVIDUALS.

*Little children, you are from God and have
overcome them, for he who is in you is greater
than he who is in the world.* ~1 John 4:4

*I can do all things through him who strength-
ens me.* ~Philippians 4:13

As the leader, it's your responsibility to empower your
team and create space for open and honest dialogue.
Using the skills of the diplomat, you lead by example.
If you're open, the team will be open. If you have the
enthusiasm and a zeal for learning, the team will catch
that enthusiasm, generating new ideas as readily as you
accept them. Of course, people want to work for
somebody who genuinely cares about them. As the
diplomat, use your heart and honor your people. When
the work gets tough, deadlines are coming, or there are
issues with the product, the team will rally behind you

and each other. This is because they are empowered to help each other be successful.

I found this to be true over the years when leading a team of people from different places. Our diversity actually allowed for quicker turnaround. Everyone shared ideas, and then they decided the way forward. The best way to empower a team is to honor their skills or grow their skills. Most people want to feel as though they are contributing and making a difference. Providing an environment where team members can contribute, no matter what level they are at creates a sense of safety. When you do this, team members are more apt to share their insights and ideas. Everyone will work together and be more efficient in such an open environment. During the challenging times of a project, the team can work out a schedule or coordinate whatever is needed to complete the task at hand. By encouraging individual growth and helping people voice their ideas and concerns, they become leaders themselves. Encouraging them to help others and to take feedback from their teammates in a safe environment builds confidence.

How do you build a safe environment? Everyone has a voice and must be heard by the whole team. In these team meetings, have each person shares something they like about the ideas being shared. With this feedback, a pilot run for a new project can be implemented. I've helped develop many processes in this way and found it to be very effective. We had different sites and small teams coming together, giving honest feedback in short time intervals to make the process as efficient as possible. Because of the diversity of the team, this actually happened quickly because different teams were using the process, and their feedback helped to finalize it. This approach worked so well we rolled out new processes more efficiently and more effectively than other disciplines. All the while, I loved working with this team. They were growing into great leaders, and it was a joy helping them become the best versions of themselves, individually and collectively. Developing people and empowering teams to be their best was my favorite part of my job.

When you build a team that can work individually and collectively without you, they are now empowered. They will move forward even without you. This is when you know you've done your job as a leader. They'll know how you think, they'll know each other, so they can figure it out. This doesn't mean they don't need you. It just means that the team is not going to fall apart if you're on vacation or you're out sick that day. By honoring who they are, they'll honor you right back.

In *"A Team Member's Guide to Project Management"* by Richard Champney and Robert Kubacki, the authors refer to a white paper published by McKinsey and Company on diversity. They discuss the financials of having diverse teams and what having diverse teams meant to the 366 different companies they researched. Diversity not only brings about positive and quick solutions it also brings about some financial gains for the company. However, it is still important to note that the work distribution should be clear for everyone.

So, from a project management perspective, everyone on the team should understand the "Iron Triangle" as Champney and Kubacki describe it. The base of the triangle is time, one leg is cost, and the other is scope. These are important to project management for planning and execution.

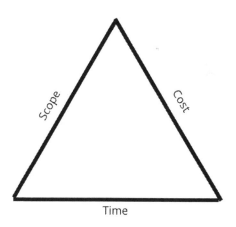

Figure 1: Iron Triangle

However, the soft skills we have been discussing in this book are also important for the success of the project. A triangle for what we've discussed so far would have communication (listen) at the base, knowledge (educate) on one side, and diversity (appreciate) on the other. See figure 1-Soft Skill Triangle. When these two triangles overlap, you have a successful, sustainable team. Your role as a leader is to implement these characteristics throughout your organization.

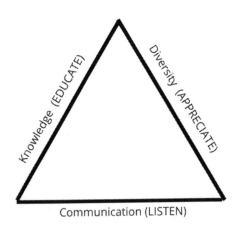

Communication (LISTEN)

Figure 2: Soft Skills Triangle

Practice Exercise 6:
Empower your Team

Think about people you would like to empower in your life.

- Generate questions to ask individuals about their personal goals and ways you can empower them to achieve those goals. Be sure to write them down.

  For example: Show interest in the goals and the achievements they've made so far whether they are big or small. Encourage them to keep going.

- What else could you do to encourage them?

Linda J. Merrill

Chapter 7

REJUVENATE

TO RESTORE TO A FORMER STATE OR
MAKE NEW AGAIN.

Come to me, all who labor and are heavy laden, and I will give you rest. Take my yoke upon you, and learn from me, for I am gentle and lowly in heart, and you will find rest for your souls. For my yoke is easy, and my burden is light. ~Matthew 11:28–30

And he said to them, "Come away by yourselves to a desolate place and rest awhile." For many were coming and going, and they had no leisure even to eat. ~Mark 6:31

There remains, then, a Sabbath-rest for the people of God; for anyone who enters God's rest also rests from their works, just as God did from his. ~Hebrews 4:9–10

Sometimes we need to rejuvenate ourselves. We can take time out from the day-to-day, or we can even to start the day by taking a deep breath. Breathe in and breathe out. Our mind, body, and soul need to rejuvenate—rebuild, regroup. When we sleep, our bodies rejuvenate. When we take the time to slow our minds down and meditate and breathe, we can usually get a picture or an image of what the future can be like. Sometimes our past issues can creep in, and we visualize the negative, but if we focus our breathing and our mind on the positive, we can see everything going right.

It takes some practice breathing and going deep within to see the positive and hold on to what's worked for yourself and for your team. But this focus brings energy. When you can recognize your team's and your own strides forward, you will have more energy to get up in the morning and do more work in an even shorter amount of time. And your team will notice your energy. They'll notice that you have time for them, that you will be able to give of yourself more freely. You can teach your team these same techniques, how to breathe in and breathe out deeply.

When you, the leader, are in a good state of mind, it is easier to listen, educate, appreciate, be a diplomat, empower, and rejuvenate the team with your enthusiasm and energy. What we think about, we bring about. Positive energy brings and gives positive energy. You cannot give what you do not have. It is important to take the time for your own personal development in order to help others do the same. You can only guide and give what you have inside of you. If you want to have energetic teams, you need to bring the energy. You need to be on board with the company mission and values and ignite them with your energy. Your enthusiasm is contagious. It's like a smile. Ever walk down the street and see someone smile at you? Do you find yourself smiling back? Why? There is an energy in a smile that is contagious, and it can be caught. Your job, in part, is to be the smile that rejuvenates your team.

The best way I've found to rejuvenate my teams is to hold workshops designed to strengthen both Soft Skills and the Iron Triangles over the course of the project. If you are a software team and using AGILE methodology, these can be done at the end of each program increment (PI), as defined by the project, to identify what worked well in the PI and what needs to be planned for the next PI. This allows for team engagement and rejuvenation during a project. Having these face-to-face meetings quarterly works best, but if that's not possible, they should minimally happen once per year. Leadership with an organization should also have quarterly face-to-face meetings and yearly strategy meetings to align and reconnect to the mission and each other.

But to best rejuvenate your team, you first must take the time to rejuvenate yourself. Jesus took the time to recharge. Why not you? Maybe you need a vacation (a real vacation—no work cell phones, no computers, no checking email). Trust your team, delegate your work, and cut ties from work for a while. The job will be there when you get back. It is harder and harder to unplug from work and easier and easier to get caught up in "I am the only one who can do the job—no one can do it like me." So not true. If you have empowered your team, they will be OK if you are gone for a little bit. In Europe, people take a month off at a time. Somehow, they keep on going. They keep on making money, and the work gets done. Don't fool yourself into thinking you are so needed you can't take a vacation.

Recharging can be done in many ways. It could be the daily practice of meditation, a massage once a week, or even going for a run or to the gym. When we clear our minds and our hearts and really let go of stress, we become better human beings. Practicing an attitude of gratitude helps as well. In 2002, I started journaling about the things I was grateful for on a regular basis. I found I saw things differently and had more peace and more to give to my family and to coworkers. By taking time at the end of each day to write out what I was grateful for or spending time with the Examen of Conscience (St. Ignatius's exercise to examine the day), I identified what I did to glorify God, where I ignored God, and when I did not live up to my potential. I was able to be more at peace, notice areas for potential improvement, and have a focus for the next day.

For the past year, I have spent time in the morning with the SAVERS from Hal Elrod's book "*The Miracle Morning*". This definitely helps to bring about peace in my soul because I spend time meditating with silence, breathing, and scripture. I reflect on what the scripture says and what it means to me for the day. This helps to charge my brain and soul, giving me what I need to lead and be at my best so I can give to others. I also take time to run in the morning before starting my day. This helps get my blood pumping and my body moving. Recharging daily and getting enough sleep is very helpful. I've studied my sleep patterns to see how much I really need to function and to feel rested when the alarm goes off. Getting up early and feeling rested creates more peace and keeps me from rushing in the morning, allowing me to promote calm not only in my home but with my team and coworkers. Then, I can lead successfully by having a clear head and being present and aware of my team's needs.

Vacations are also important for my own rejuvenation, but I also encouraged my team to take vacations. Some people need an extra push to allow themselves to rejuvenate their bodies and souls and spend time with their families. I also encouraged team members to leave work at a reasonable time in the evening. They are no good to the company or the team if members overwork themselves and get sick. When the team is rested and has time to recharge, it helps the individual, the team, and the company. By leading and encouraging everyone to take care of him or herself, I found everyone would pitch in when someone was out of the office. The work didn't slip because we built a system of communication, and everyone was rejuvenated.

Practice Exercise 7:
Rejuvenate

Make a list of vacation ideas for yourself.

- Engage your family or the people you want to travel with.

- Look at your calendar and schedule either the current year's vacation or a weekend getaway.

- On the following page, make your list and choose together where you will go and when. Write down the dates and the cost so you can plan.

Chapter 8

SUPPORT

TO PROP UP, SUSTAIN, OR KEEP
FUNCTIONING.

*Whatever you do, work at it with all your heart,
as working for the Lord, not for human
masters, since you know that you will receive
an inheritance from the Lord as a reward. It is
the Lord Christ you are serving.*
                              ~Colossians 3:23–24

The most successful projects I've been on started with a
clear plan. I don't just mean a schedule. Schedules are
great to keep you on task, but I'm talking about a
comprehensive plan—including a development plan, a
distribution plan, and a communication plan. It should
be clear how all the teams work together, where their
communication links are, how you're going to develop
your product, and where the lead manufacturing site is.
All of this needs to be established at the beginning of
your project. Workshops held quarterly are a great way

to plan and check in to ensure the project is on track, but the best and most successful projects hold these workshops (kickoffs) at the beginning.

These meetings also help the team members know what is expected of them. They help keep everyone on track and are great ways to build relationships with the team. Each team member should have an opportunity to give input in the planning and build working relationships with each other. Technical knowledge is certainly important, but the most successful teams have built a solid foundation of good communication, knowledge, and experience with each other. These relationships are important because team members who trust each other work better together. By building trust and working together, you as the leader can better support the needs of the team members and remove obstacles in the workflow. In other words, you want to build a system that sustains itself.

As we learned with the Iron Triangle of project management and the Soft Skills Triangle, leadership and management go hand in hand. How these triangles overlap is key to a successful team. Not only do you have to manage the project, but the team also has to be led to success. Learning the soft skills encompassed by LEADERS will ensure the success of co-located teams or even teams sitting in the same facility.

Co-located teams and diverse teams naturally create opportunities for innovation. Even if you're following a plan, when you have different types of people in your program, ideas emerge that could not have grown in isolated, non-diverse groups. When people of different backgrounds communicate and work together well, they can figure out how to streamline processes when they realize how things are working. They will have moments where they say, "Oh, wait a minute. I don't need to do this because that person is doing it already." With proper communication channels in place, nothing gets missed, and overlap is reduced or eliminated.

It's actually very exciting to watch what diverse teams can generate. By keeping an open mind and allowing for communication, people's differences actually fuel camaraderie and innovation within your teams. As a leader, you look good because your team is performing, and the team feels like they've contributed so much that they want to be successful together. It's just a win-win for everybody.

Even with this groundwork in place, however, you still need to find ways to sustain and support your team. I found that regularly asking team members if they needed anything from me did wonders for this. This helped me know the obstacles that might be holding them back from doing their job, and then I could try to work out solutions to address those obstacles. By listening to them in this way, I encouraged them to ask me, the project manager, or technical leads questions when they felt they needed information or guidance for their work.

Sustaining my teams also meant striving to support team members in all areas of their lives. I would find out what they loved to do and engage them in short conversations about their family, friends, and weekends. Remember, be interested in the whole person. By finding out what my team members liked to do or the places they'd visited, I could see what was important to them and support them to meet those external goals—in addition to their work goals. When they were happy, I was happy. And when an employee is happy, they want to stay.

When you know what's important to someone, you know what brings them the most joy. For some, it could be the chance to dive into their work. Those people want to grow and learn as much as they can for work. For others, motivation to work is all about the paycheck. To keep employees engaged and have retention, it's important for them to feel valued and heard by you. The same goes for you as the manager/leader too. You want to ensure that you're meeting their needs while meeting your own personal and work goals. Everyone wants to accomplish their goals, whether it be accomplishing something at work, taking lots of trips, or owning a home. As a leader, you want to help those working for you realize those goals through their work, which will help them feel fulfilled. When people are happy to work for you, they'll want to stay.

This was true of a coworker I had who had said to me several times that he stayed with the company because he liked working for me. At first, I was like, "Yeah, yeah. Sure, whatever. You're just saying that." But he elaborated and explained that the work, although challenging, did not feel like work. So, how did I do that? Again, asking questions about his family, about his kids, and about things he liked to do, but also by supporting him when there were issues, by supporting him when the work got really, really tough, and by acknowledging that we all struggle. This happened by having a real relationship, not something superficial.

It wasn't that I had it all together or that so-and-so had it all together. No, it was that we kept it real. There were tough parts of the job, and acknowledging that and having everyone's back made it possible to work through them. This also meant having their back even if their idea wasn't the one we used. Input is always valuable, and even if we didn't use someone's idea, I would not throw them under the bus and say, "No, no, no. We're not going to do that." Instead, I would say something like, "You know what? Let's take a step back. Let's look at all the facts, and then we'll make a decision." Offline I would ask them to tell me how they arrived to that conclusion. I would ask for data, for facts, for reasons. Then we would decide which way to go. This helped them feel heard while still grounding decisions in facts and data, no gut feelings. And of course, my mind could change once all the data was on the table.

Offline conversations allow employees to be heard and understand that I am supporting them no matter what, and even if their solutions weren't the right ones, we would work through how to get to the correct decision without others observing. Sometimes a group of our own quality team would join the conversation, but not other managers or other teams. These smaller groups made sure these coaching or mentoring sessions had value. They also allowed the younger engineers to learn and share their thought processes so everyone on the team could have the same understanding. If a similar situation arose before a delivery or a software or product launch, it was then easier for everybody to come to the same conclusions. Overall, this process ensured employee retention since people knew they could grow in the company and that I had their back.

The biggest gift you can give to anyone is the gift of human dignity. When you allow your team members to be who they are and allow them to learn and grow, you give them the gift of self-discovery and the chance to become the best versions of themselves. An integral part of being a leader is to help your people develop both professionally and personally. One of the fruits of my labor was watching my team grow as individuals and as a team.

Amazingly, I saw this at a spiritual level. We came from so many different backgrounds. There were Catholics, people from other Christian denominations, people of Jewish faith, Muslims, agnostics, Buddhists, and people who didn't believe in anything but were still spiritual. We were all able to talk about our faiths and still support each other professionally, personally, and spiritually. I would talk with my wonderful Muslim colleagues about their holidays and what they meant to them. During Ramadan, I would pray for them, and they would pray for me. This openness and willingness to discuss our faiths, even across faith traditions, fostered our team's camaraderie, generated amazing conversations, and gave us new ways of understanding and relating to each other.

What I found is that when you're engaged with your team, when there's a connection, when there's openness, employees really want to do a good job, and they want to stay where they are. They also want to grow in their position, feel trusted, and hear they're doing a good job. Recognition is huge, and I don't mean monetary recognition. I mean honoring who they are and the work they do, all in an honest, thoughtful way. You can't just say, "Oh, thanks," as we automatically do when somebody passes the salt and pepper. Show genuine appreciation for their work. By honoring them in this way, you give them dignity, and employee retention will happen organically. When employees feel they contribute to the organization, doing the work has meaning, and they will want to stay. So, it's really important to hear them and see where they're coming from, what they're doing, and where they want to go. It's all about honoring them as human beings.

It's way too easy for humanity to be taken out of the job. We have robotics in the production lines. We have computers that do much of the work. People order their coffee through an app and may not even go inside the coffee shop to pick it up. There seems to be a drive-thru for everything. We even have drive-thru pharmacies. But amid all of this, I have found that people are starved for human connection—real connection.

You can have a great relationship with your employees without being all buddy-buddy and hanging out with them on the weekends. It is all about the human connection and showing you care about who they are. When you're connected on a level that allows for open, honest communication and appreciation for who they are and the work that they've performed, they feel it and want to stay working for you.

Working in such an open environment also means not always taking yourself too seriously. I would often laugh at myself or something stupid I did to ease tensions and make work not always feel like work. Likewise, we would work hard for an hour or two, and then we would take a five or ten-minute break. We would let off some steam by talking about something else or going for a walk to get a coffee. Before we knew it, we would all start laughing as we talked about something that happened the night before or a joke someone told. The team was a team, in good times and in bad. We were always there to support each other.

This happened, in part, because we always included everyone. It is really important to be inclusive. People want to feel part of something, and if your shared mission is bigger than the problems and the issues going on in the daily work, the bonds within the team will strengthen. By being inclusive of everyone, you create possibilities for your teammates, and when that possibility is communicated clearly, they work to make it a reality.

And there is your retention. Your employees will stay and see collective goals come to fruition. They will want to stay so they can work for an employer who genuinely cares about them. Leading from the heart in this way is key when you're a manager and have people working for you. They really want to know that you care about their whole being. When my employees had something going on at home, I made sure to allow them to work from home on those days. My expectation was always that their family came first. The work had to get done too, of course, but I trusted they would figure out how to manage their time wisely and still meet deadlines, even if they had to use other personal time.

If you're working with international teams while located in the US, starting work at home early morning to communicate overseas can also be an advantage. I don't think anyone on my team missed these kinds of early morning meetings (mid-morning for Europe), and the meetings were productive. Doing this allowed US employees to be done earlier in the day, which also helped to keep them around. If there were major deadlines, they would stay later and then leave early on Friday or another day. This policy benefited both the employee and the company since the work was getting done on time while allowing for work-life balance. If an employee feels like their whole life has to revolve around the company, then that can cause problems at home, especially if they have a family. Then you might lose your employee. This is why I love the philosophy of faith first, family second, career third. This does not mean you don't show up to work. On the contrary, it means that you put your priorities in line and then can be more productive at work.

Mary Kay Ash, founder of Mary Kay cosmetics, was a member of the five o'clock club. She woke up at 5:00 a.m., which allowed her to have her quiet time for scripture reading and journaling before her family was up. I also have found this practice to be beneficial, allowing me to have a clearer head and to be more productive and present with my family and while at work. I encouraged all my employees to do the same. By encouraging them to spend time in quiet and to make sure they addressed their family needs, I helped my employees feel cared for, and they in turn were more willing do what was needed for the job around their family needs. Of course, they would need to attend meetings essential to their roles or find someone to cover, but the work did get done, and they were genuinely happy.

Many larger companies today offer work-from-home options or job sharing. This may be in an effort to ensure proper work-life balance or because the office has minimal space. When office space is at a premium, people share offices and work out a schedule so that only one of them is in the office at a time. This is happening more and more, but working from home instead of at the office is not always possible and depends on the job. But if the employees can still get their work done on time, it's reasonable to have some leeway.

But how do a leader and manager handle illness? I sometimes had massive migraines, and I couldn't go to the office when I felt that way. I would have to sleep off the migraine and then be hyper-focused once it was gone. If the headache came back, I would just lie down again. If it didn't really go away, but I could function, then I would work.

Some of your employees may have similar health difficulties, and it can be a benefit to allow them to stay home so they can have the flexibility when they really need it. When there's an understanding or a written document that allows for this flexibility (as long as it's not abused), employees are often much happier to go above and beyond in their work. When you allow for this kind of flexibility, you provide for their needs, and they provide better work performance.

I had a very high-performing team because of this kind of flexibility. Most of the time, everyone got their work done, and many times they went above and beyond, even when working from home, tending to a sick child, or attending a softball game. Again, when you allow people to prioritize their faith and family above their career, it helps them perform and make them want to stay.

I know it may be strange to talk about choosing faith and family first, especially in the United States, where it's work, work, work, and career, career, career. But in reality, people have priorities that aren't necessarily in line with just work, work, work. Sure, there are workaholics and people who find their worth in their work, but most people don't see their careers as the most important aspect of their life. I have found that when people in the workplace are able to align their lives around faith, family, and then career, overall performance is higher, retention is higher, and there's a peacefulness that exists even in the chaos.

The key to supporting employees in this way is to be open and make the work as light as possible. I don't mean make the workload light—just make sure people feel free to be themselves without getting bogged down in the seriousness of the work. Things will get serious sometimes, but that doesn't mean you have to take every single day so seriously. Work hard and play hard. Not taking yourself too seriously can help people feel relaxed and make the workplace peaceful, joyful, and productive all at once.

There is no better gift to give to somebody than to allow them to grow into who they're meant to be. When you can do that with your teams, you will have higher retention. If they leave the company, and the relationship is still good, you never know—they may return, or they will send people who are a good fit. I still talk to my team. I love them with all my heart. They became part of my heart and my family. When we build relationships in the workplace that are healthy, honest and full of integrity, teams are more apt to keep working together. Life needs your team, but if you provide a space for growth, your company and team will thrive.

Practice Exercise 8:
Support

On the next page, make a list of ways you can support your team or your family.

- Think of ways to help them be successful or back them up when they need it. Refer to this list often.

- Can you create time or provide resources for them to continue their education? Can you cover for them when they are on vacation?

- When making your list, think of each team member and consider what they might need or desire to know that you are supporting them.

Conclusion

Your word is a lamp to my feet and a light to my path. ~Psalm 119:105

Have I not commanded you? Be strong and courageous. Do not be frightened, and do not be dismayed, for the Lord your God is with you wherever you go. ~Joshua 1:9

We have been talking about LEADERS. Let's recap:

L is for Listen. Take the time to listen to your people and coworkers. Ask lots of questions and always be curious. This enables communication and open, honest dialogue for your team. It may not always be easy to listen when we think that we already know something or know more than the person speaking, but listening is a soft skill worth learning. A good practice when asking questions is to pretend you are a journalist writing down the facts of what a person is saying in order to go to print. This will allow you to really hear them and open up more questions. When you take the time to listen to your team members individually or collectively, you create a safe space to share with you, or with each other, their needs, concerns, and ideas.

E is for Educate. You can educate yourself in many ways—by reading, researching, by going to school, and again, by asking questions. When you take the time to educate yourself about your team, your work, roles and expectations, customer requirements, financials, etc., you give yourself and your team the knowledge necessary to be successful. Allowing your team to become educated and providing the tools they need for their role and their aspirations set them up for success. When the team is successful, they look good, which means you look good.

A is for Appreciate. When you appreciate your team as a whole and as individual members in an honest and grateful way, you help them to grow. You value them as humans and as contributors whose work matters to you and to the company. This appreciation does not need to be manifest financially, but it could be if the company allows for that type of recognition. By appreciating honestly, even without money, you are valuing their work and all they put into the job. If you do this, team members are more apt to continue to work hard and provide you with excellent work.

Additionally, when you appreciate the diversity of cultures and embrace the differences that everyone brings to the team, the members become more cohesive and learn from each other. As the leader, you should exemplify what being appreciative and grateful looks like for each team member, thereby promoting acceptance to the whole team. The team members can then learn from each other and grow together.

D is for Diplomat. Being the bridge for your team between different departments gives your team the freedom to work and be autonomous. You provide a safety zone for them. Understanding your team dynamics and providing open dialogue to bring them together toward a common goal or mission creates a sense of camaraderie. As a result, the whole human system will work better together. When teams are diverse or co-located, being a diplomat is key to clear, open, honest communication. By understanding how different cultures communicate and work, you can support the team and bring peace when there are misunderstandings.

E is for Empower. When you have enthusiasm for your work and for your team members, and there is a mission bigger than the work at hand, the team will be more apt to work hard to complete the tasks needed. Allowing the team to create their mission both collectively and individually provides purpose for the work. People want to feel like they are part of something bigger than themselves. When they collectively understand or create this purpose, they will do what it takes to meet it.

R is for Rejuvenate. Make sure you take the time for yourself and let your team do the same. By taking vacations with your family or time away for yourself to recharge, you will be a better manager. Your team members should also have the privilege to step away and be with their families or by themselves to recharge. You can also hold team-building workshops away from the day-to-day to rejuvenate the purpose and mission of the work and to come together to solve a problem. This helps the team to recharge their excitement and keeps them connected to the purpose.

S is for Support. To keep employees engaged in their work and happy to come in every day, the mission needs to be bigger than the problems at hand. Work doesn't need to feel like work if everyone feels empowered and appreciated. The team will want to stay when they have a purpose and are working toward something bigger than themselves.

All of these soft skills are an important part of managing a team. Even if you are not a manager, these skills can help you grow your own career. When you can master these skills, you will have successful teams and provide leadership that others will want to follow.

Acknowledgments

A huge thank you to my coach at Self-Publishing School Lise Cartwright for her invaluable knowledge and guidance throughout the whole process of writing to final book and her patience with me as I stumbled through.

I also want to thank my team from Valeo for giving me the opportunity to lead and learn and grow as their manager and for their trust in me. Their love and inspiration helped me to write this book.

To Qat Wanders and her team of editors at Elite Publishing for their flexibility and expertise in helping me get to the final product. Nina Pierce who has been so amazing to work with over the course of writing as a resource and for formatting the book for me. (Thanks cousin!). To Dar Albert of Wicked Smart Designs for an amazing book cover especially with so little direction. You totally ROCK!!

Karen and John Manelas for letting me use their lake house to sit quiet, write and self-edit the final draft to send to editing.

Of course, my family for their patience and support as I worked through the writing process. For my son Alex to reading the manuscript and providing a few more updates. I appreciate each and every one of you for your endless support and encouragement. I am eternally grateful.

What's next??

For professional or personal development,
please visit my website:

PontemVitae.com

Or get more information by emailing me:

info@pontemvitae.com

Please visit my website to receive your
FREE copy of my companion workbook

PontemVitae.com

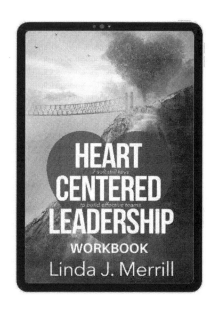

About the Author

Linda has been married to her husband, Michael for over twenty-six years. They have three sons. She loves to visit churches for the beauty, peace, and history. She has traveled to many different countries in her thirty-year career in the technology industry and has encount-ered countless fascinating people and places along the way. Linda found her niche of leading diverse international teams while working as a global system and software quality manager at Valeo. Known for being a social butterfly, she enjoys spending time with family and friends.

Can You Help?

Thank You for Reading My Book!

I really appreciate all of your feedback, and I love hearing what you have to say. I need your input to make the next version of this book and my future books better. Please leave me an honest review on Amazon letting me know what you thought of the book.

Thanks so much!

Made in the USA
Lexington, KY
21 December 2019

58786047R00061